COLUMBIA

COMMON ENGLISH USAGE MISTAKES AT LPI™

Richard Lee, Ph.D.

COLUMBIA PRESS

Copyright © 2012 Richard Lee, Columbia Press

All rights reserved.

No part of this book may be reproduced or distributed in any form or by any menans without the written permission of the copyright owner.

All inquiries should be addressed to:

Columbia Press

803-470 Granville Street

Vancouver, BC V6C 1V5

ISBN-13: 978-0-9880191-8-8

To Nancy S. T. , Philip, T. L., and Christina K. L

CONTENTS

INTRODUCTION   ix

CHAPTER ONE: INCORRECT USE OF AN ARTICLE   11

Lesson 1   Testing Point: Use Articles Correctly   12

Lesson 2   Testing Point: Confusion of Articles: Distinguish Between Specific and General Ideas   15

CHAPTER TWO: INCORRECT NUMBER OF A NOUN   19

Lesson 3   Testing Point: Use the Correct Singular or Plural Noun   20

CHAPTER THREE: INCORRECT USE OF A PRONOUN   24

Lesson 4   Testing Point: Use Personal, Possessive , and Reflexive Pronouns Correctly   25

Lesson 5   Use Reflexive Pronouns Correctly   28

CHAPTER FOUR: INCORRECT USE OF A VERB   31

Lesson 6 Testing Point: Problems with Passive Verbs   32

Lesson 7 Testing Point: Use *Have* + Past Participle and *Had* + Past Participle Correctly   35

Lesson 8 Testing Point: Emphasis: Nouns Derived from Subjunctive Verbs   39

Lesson 9 Testing Point: Invert the Subject and Verb with Conditionals   43

Lesson 10 Testing Point: Errors with Verbals   46

Lesson 11 Testing Point: Problems with Infinitives   50

CHAPTER FIVE: ADVERB AND ADJECTIVE CONFUSION   54

Lesson 12 Testing Point: Use Basic Adjectives and Adverbs Correctly   55

CHAPTER SIX: INCORRECT USE OF A PREPOSITION   59

Lesson 13 Testing Point: Recognize Incorrect Prepositions and Prepositional Phrases   60

Lesson 14 Testing Point: Errors with Prepositions   63

CHAPTER SEVEN: FAULTY DICTION   67

Lesson 15 Testing Point: Use *Borrow* and *Lend*, *Let* and *Leave* Correctly   68

Lesson 16 Testing Point: Use *A little* and *Little, A Few* and *Few* Correctly 73

CHAPTER EIGHT: NON-STANDARD WORDS, EXPRESSIONS, OR IDIOMS 77

Lesson 17 Testing Point: Check Word Form: Words That Don't Exist in English 78

CHAPTER NINE: INCORRECT DEGREE OF COMPARISON 81

Lesson 18 Testing Point: Check Equative, Comparative, and Superlative Degree 82

Lesson 19 Testing Point: Comparative Estimates: *More Than* and *Less Than* 86

CHAPTER TEN: CONFUSION BETWEEN WORDS WITH SIMILAR SOUNDS (HOMOPHONES OR NEAR-HOMOPHONES) 89

Lesson 20 Testing Point: Use Words with Similar Sounds Correctly 90

Acknowledgements 99

ABOUT THE AUTHOR 101

INTRODUCTION

Columbia Common English Usage Mistakes at LPI is compiled to help you learn the absolutely essential grammar testing points and avoid the most common mistakes at LPI to raise your score! It has twenty lessons with each one having the following outstanding features:

- <u>ERROR EXAMPLES</u>: show you what kinds of mistakes most often made at LPI and how to correct them;
- <u>GRAMMAR GUIDES</u>: teach you the grammar rules absolutely essential to raise your LPI score;
- <u>PRACTICE TESTS</u>: Use sample Sentence Correction and Sentence Completion questions to test your grammar power and readiness for the real LPI;
- <u>ANSWER KEYS</u>: provide answers and explanations to help you avoid the mistakes forever to score higher on the LPI!

Columbia Common English Usage Mistakes at LPI is your grammar Bible! With the help of our fun and effective way to learn all the essential grammar testing points, you will be able to score higher on the LPI guaranteed!

CHAPTER ONE

INCORRECT USE OF AN ARTICLE

LESSON 1

TESTING POINT: USE ARTICLES CORRECTLY

ERROR EXAMPLE

WRONG: That's such a deep question. Yeah. Is a virtual world likely to be an Utopia, would be one way I'd say it.

RIGHT: That's such a deep question. Yeah. Is a virtual world likely to be <u>a</u> Utopia, would be one way I'd say it.

GRAMMAR GUIDE

In English, there are two kinds of articles: indefinite artices *a* and *an* and definite artice *the*.

For indefinite Articles, the basic difference between *a* and *an* is that *a* is used in front of consonants and *an* is used in front of vowels {a, e, i, o, u).

WRONG: It is an universal fact that we have only one earth.

RIGHT: It is a universal fact that we have only one earth.

The definite article *the* is used with singular and plural nouns or the nouns referring to things we already know about.

WRONG: Michael Blake is a player you can count on for success.

RIGHT: Michael Blake is the player you can count on for success.

PRACTICE TEST

Test 1. SENTENCE COMPLETION: Choose the CORRECT answer.

1. The scholarship that Philip received to study finance at Harvard University presented_____.

   A. a unique opportunity

   B. an unique opportunity

2. _____ responds to a wide range of frequencies.

   A. An human ear

   B..A human ear

Test 2. SENTENCE CORRECTION: Choose the INCORRECT word or phrase and CORRECT it.

1. We went to the store and bought new stove.

2. It is always difficult to make the decisions.

3. She doesn't have understanding of the subject yet.

4. Dogs make the good pets.

5. The honesty is a virtue.

ANSWER KEY

Test 1:

1. A (use *an* only with words beginning with a vowel sound)

2. B (use *an* only with words beginning with a vowel sound)

Test 2:

1. We went to the store and bought <u>a</u> new stove.

2. It is always difficult to <u>make decisions</u>.

3. She doesn't have <u>an</u> understanding of the subject yet.

4. Dogs make <u>good pets</u>.

5. <u>Honesty</u> is a virtue.

LESSON 2

TESTING POINT: CONFUSION OF ARTICLES: DISTINGUISH BETWEEN SPECIFIC AND GENERAL IDEAS

ERROR EXAMPLE

WRONG: Channel 4 said an experiment had a scientific purpose and had not been done for sensationalism.

RIGHT: Channel 4 said the experiment had a scientific purpose and had not been done for sensationalism.

GRAMMAR GUIDE

Both indefinite articles *a* and *an* and definite article *the* can be used before a singular countable noun. However, the definite article *the* refers to something specific or something we already know while indefinite articles *a* and *an* refer to something not specific or something we don't know exactly.

WRONG: Dr. Edward Johnson, the Dean of our college, is a person I want to see this afternoon.

RIGHT: Dr. Edward Johnson, the Dean of our college, is <u>the</u> person I want to see this afternoon.

WRONG: We went crab fishing on the chartered boat near Georgia Strait last Sunday.

RIGHT: We went crab fishing on <u>a</u> chartered boat near Georgia Strait last Sunday.

PRACTICE TEST

Test 1. SENTENCE COMPLETION: Choose the CORRECT answer.

1. Soil is composed of_____organic matter called humus and inorganic matter derived from rocks.

   A. the mixture of

   B. a mixture

2. A professor from Yale University will be giving_____at the Student Union building on Friday.

   A. a speech

   B. the speech

Test 2. SENTENCE CORRECTION: Choose the INCORRECT word or phrase and CORRECT it.

1. Alvin is a monitor of our English conversation class.

2. Seattle is considered only city in the North West that has the best climate.

3. My hometown is a place that has four clear seasons.

4. The university is where we can receive a more advanced education.

5. My grandpa's Snake Farm is a most exciting place I have ever been to in the world.

ANSWER KEY

Test 1:

1. B (Here *a* should be used because nothing specific is being mentioned.)

2. A (Here we use indefinite article *a* because the speech is not being specifically known to us.)

Test 2:

1. Alvin is the monitor of our English conversation class.

2. Seattle is considered the only city in the North West that has the best climate.

3. My hometown is the place that has four clear seasons.

4. A university is where we can receive a more advanced education.

5. My grandpa's Snake Farm is <u>the</u> most exciting place I have ever been to in the world.

CHAPTER TWO

INCORRECT NUMBER OF A NOUN

LESSON 3

TESTING POINT: USE THE CORRECT SINGULAR OR PLURAL NOUN

ERROR EXAMPLE

WRONG: Before you bet the bank on your next million dollars idea, you should do a reality check to see if the idea is worth it.

RIGHT: Before you bet the bank on your next <u>million dollar</u> idea, you should do a reality check to see if the idea is worth it.

GRAMMAR GUIDE

One of the most common mistakes at English tests is that a singular noun is used where a plural noun is needed, or a plural noun is used where a singular noun is needed.

Remember that after these key words, *each, every, a, one,* and *single,* a singular noun is used.

WRONG: With a few exceptions, the benchmark cost of credit in each euro-zone countries is related to the balance of its international debts.

RIGHT: With a few exceptions, the benchmark cost of credit in <u>each</u> euro-zone <u>country</u> is related to the balance of its international debts.

Be careful that after these words, *many, several, both, various,* and *two,* plural nouns should be used.

WRONG: The auto shop has many parts for various type of expensive European cars.

RIGHT: The auto shop has many parts for <u>various types</u> of expensive European cars.

WRONG: On advices from his doctor, Michael Jones finally gave up smoking.

RIGHT: On <u>advice</u> from his doctor, Michael Jones finally gave up smoking.

PRACTICE TEST

Test 1. SENTENCE COMPLETION: Choose the CORRECT answer.

1. A U.S president can only serve a maximum of two_____.

   A. four-years terms

   B. four-year term

2. _____ were very upset after they had learned of the tuition increase next year.

   A. A number of student

   B. A number of students

Test 2. SENTENCE CORRECTION: Choose the INCORRECT word or phrase and CORRECT it.

1. Both of my friend are going to Australia to study this fall.

2. Each of the committee member voiced his opinion.

3. Every student should bear his responsibilities to be a good citizen.

4. One of the candidate wants to hold a public debate on campus safety.

5. A number of student activist have voted to establish a poverty fund for college students.

ANSWER KEY

Test 1:

1. B (Here it should be *four-year* instead of *four-years* because when a noun is used as an adjective, it should be in the singular form.)

2. B (After *a number of*, always use plural noun.)

Test 2:

1. Both of my <u>friends</u> are going to Australia to study this fall.

2. Each of the committee <u>members</u> voiced his opinion.

3. Every student should bear his <u>responsibility</u> to be a good citizen.

4. One of the <u>candidates</u> wants to hold a public debate on campus safety.

5. A number of student <u>activists</u> have voted to establish a poverty fund for college students. (Here *student* is a noun used as an adjective modifying activists; therefore, it should be singular)

CHAPTER THREE

INCORRECT USE OF A PRONOUN

LESSON 4

TESTING POINT: USE PERSONAL, POSSESSIVE, AND REFLEXIVE PRONOUNS CORRECTLY

ERROR EXAMPLE

WRONG: "Everybody should weigh their words very carefully. What we do not need is alarm in financial markets," she said

RIGHT: "Everybody should weigh his words very carefully. What we do not need is alarm in financial markets," she said

GRAMMAR GUIDE

Pronouns are used to replace or refer to nouns, gerunds, infinitives, and sometimes entire clauses. Pronouns change form depending on their functions in sentences.

Remember that always check personal, possessive, and reflexive pronouns for agreement.

WRONG: Nobody should be judged by their appearance.

RIGHT: Nobody should be judged by his appearance.

WRONG: We must let all citizens know his rights and obligations in the society.

RIGHT: We must let all citizens know their rights and obligations in the society.

PRACTICE TEST

Test 1. SENTENCE COMPLETION: Choose the CORRECT answer.

1. Everyone must sign_____at the reception desk.

   A. their name

   B. his name

2. He is one of those people who always_____.

   A. brag about themselves

   B. brag about himself

Test 2. SENTENCE CORRECTION: Choose the INCORRECT word or phrase and CORRECT it.

1. Between you and I, the economic situation does not look bad.

2. It was him who knocked on the door last night.

3. Jack is as tall as me.

4. You don't have to worry about me. I can cook myself my dinner.

5. It is she, the one whom nobody likes.

ANSWER KEY

Test 1:

1.B (Here *everyone* is the third person singular, therefore, the possessive pronoun should be *his*.)

2. A (Here you should use reflexive pronoun *themselves* because it refres to *people*.)

Test 2:

1. Between you and me, the economic situation does not look bad.

2. It was he who knocked on the door last night.

3. Jack is as tall as I.

4. You don't have to worry about me. I can cook dinner myself.

5. It is her, the one whom nobody likes.

LESSON 5

TESTING POINT: USE REFLEXIVE PRONOUNS CORRECTLY

ERROR EXAMPLE

WRONG: The best ones can take a good idea and use it to transform itself from embryos into giants in a few years, as Amazon and Google have.

RIGHT: The best ones can take a good idea and use it to transform themselves from embryos into giants in a few years, as Amazon and Google have.

GRAMMAR GUIDE

In English, a reflexive pronoun (*myself, ourselves, yourself, yourselves, himself, herself, themselves, itself*) can be used as the complement of a sentence or a clause. It can also be used as the object of a preposition.

WRONG: When you take a test, you should always give you enough time to check the answers before you hand it in.

RIGHT: When you take a test, you should always give <u>yourself</u> enough time to check the answers before you hand it in.

WRONG: It seems everyone knows favouritism exists — but nobody wants to put his hand up and say he is guilty of it itself.

RIGHT: It seems everyone knows favouritism exists — but nobody wants to put his hand up and say he is guilty of it <u>himself</u>.

PRACTICE TEST

Test 1. SENTENCE COMPLETION: Choose the CORRECT answer.

1. According to the Fifth Amendment to the U.S. Constitution, nobody should be compelled to be a witness_____.

   A. against themselves

   B. against himself

2. All this would be apart from the failure of two generations of efforts to build a strong European framework_____.

   A. around Germany themselves.

   B. around Germany itself.

Test 2. SENTENCE CORRECTION: Choose the INCORRECT word or phrase and CORRECT it.

1. Be careful with these sharp tools or you will hurt to you.

2. A child can usually feed self by the age of six months.

3. Since nobody knew how to swim in my family, I had to teach me how to swim.

4. Help you to whatever you like, it is free.

5. A modern microwave that can clean it is really unbelievable.

ANSWER KEY

Test 1:

1. B (Here *nobody* is the third person singular, therefore, *itself* should be used here.)

2. B (Here *Germany* is the third person singular, therefore, *itself* should be used here.)

Test 2:

1. Be careful with these sharp tools or you will hurt <u>yourself</u>.

2. A child can usually feed <u>himself</u> by the age of six months.

3. Since nobody knew how to swim in my family, I had to teach <u>myslef</u> how to swim.

4. Help <u>yourself</u> to whatever you like, it is free.

5. A modern microwave that can clean <u>itself</u> is really unbelievable.

CHAPTER FOUR

INCORRECT USE OF A VERB

LESSON 6

TESTING POINT: PROBLEMS WITH PASSIVE VERBS

ERROR EXAMPLE

WRONG: The causes of the disaster are due not to faulty organization, but to the misfortune in all risks which have to undertake.

RIGHT: The causes of the disaster are due not to faulty organization, but to the misfortune in all risks which have to <u>be undertaken.</u>

GRAMMAR GUIDE

Sentences in which the error is an incorrect passive or active are common in English tests. Therefore, you must be able to determine whether a passive verb (passive voice) rather than an active verb (active voice) is needed in a sentence and vice versa.

WRONG: Nobody should judge by his wallet.

RIGHT: Nobody <u>should be judged</u> by his wallet.

WRONG: A mystery is something that can't explain.

RIGHT: A mystery is something that <u>can't be explained.</u>

PRACTICE TEST

Test 1. SENTENCE COMPLETION: Choose the CORRECT answer.

1. The answer_____ by most of the students in our class.

    A. was knew

    B. was known

2. Your laptop would not_____ if you had not left it on the back seat of your car.

    A. have been stolen

    B. have stolen

Test 2. SENTENCE CORRECTION: Choose the INCORRECT word or phrase and CORRECT it.

1. Another man was being hired for the position yesterday.

2. A high-tech park is going to build near the university city.

3. I Have never been informed of his coming before he came.

4. All the building are been destroyed during the bombing.

5. We were gave a prize by the school district.

ANSWER KEY

Test 1:

1. B (Here passive voice *was known*, not *was knew*.)

2. A (Here passive voice *have been stolen* must be used.)

Test 2:

1. Another man <u>was hired</u> for the position yesterday.

2. A high-tech park is going <u>to be built</u> near the university city.

3. I <u>had never been informed</u> of his coming before he came.

4. All the buildings <u>were destroyed</u> during the bombing.

5. We <u>were given</u> a prize by the school district.

LESSON 7

TESTING POINT: USE *HAVE* + PAST PARTICIPLE AND *HAD* + PAST PARTICIPLE CORRECTLY

ERROR EXAMPLE

WRONG: We would accomplish the task much earlier if you had come to help us.

RIGHT: We would have accomplished the task much earlier if you had come to help us.

GRAMMAR GUIDE

The Present Perfect Tense (*have* + past participle) and the Past Perfect Tense (*had* + past participle) have completely different uses.

The present perfect refers to something happened in the past and continued to present. At the time of speaking, the action is completed.

WRONG: William Black lived in Vancouver for almost twenty years.

RIGHT: William Black has lived in Vancouver for almost twenty years.

WRONG: At the start of the twenty-first century, cell phones have become very popular among teenagers.

RIGHT: At the start of the twenty-first century, cell phones became very popular among teenagers.

The past perfect refers to something that had been completed before something happened in the past.

WRONG: Jennifer has finished her dinner when Jack came to pick her up.

RIGHT: Jennifer had finished her dinner when Jack came to pick her up.

WRONG: Mary already went to sleep when we arrived.

RIGHT: Mary had already gone to sleep when we arrived.

PRACTICE TEST

Test 1. SENTENCE COMPLETION: Choose the CORRECT answer.

1. If I _____ billion dollars when I was young, I would have married a Hollywood star.

   A. had a

   B. had had a

2. Had I known you at Harvard Business School, we _____.

   A. would become business partners

   B. would have become business partners

Test 2. SENTENCE CORRECTION: Choose the INCORRECT word or phrase and CORRECT it.

1. After I complete my studies in America, I will return to my own country.

2. When she began her schooling, she has already memorized 3000 new words.

3. Since I am grown up now, I should help my parents in finances.

4. Up to now, the city had built five community centres.

5. By the end of 1988, the number of students in the country risen to 12 million.

ANSWER KEY

Test 1:

1. B (Here past perfect tense *had had* should be used in the adverbial clause of condition; for in the main clause, we use past future perfect tense *would have married*.)

2. B (Here in the adverbial clause of past conditional, it is the past perfect tense, therefore, in the main clause, it should be past future perfect tense: *would have become*.)

Test 2:

1. After I have completed my studies in America, I will return to my own country.

2. When she began her schooling, she had already memorized 3000 new words.

3. Since I have grown up now, I should help my parents in finances.

4. Up to now, the city has built five community centres.

5. By the end of 1988, the number of students in the country had risen to 12 million.

LESSON 8

TESTING POINT:

EMPHASIS: NOUNS DERIVED FROM SUBJUNCTIVE VERBS

ERROR EXAMPLE

WRONG: Council agrees in general to the recommendation that the condition for the dependant to live with the applicant is relaxed.

RIGHT: Council agrees in general to the recommendation that the condition for the dependant to live with the applicant <u>be relaxed.</u>

GRAMMAR GUIDE

Remember that the following nouns derived from subjunctive verbs are most often used in this pattern:

demand, insistenc, preference, proposal, recommendation, request requirement, suggestion:

WRONG: Mary Jones thought the editor's insistence that she makes clear that the story was a spoof was unnecessary.

RIGHT: Mary Jones thought the editor's insistence that she <u>make</u> clear that the story was a spoof was unnecessary.

WRONG: But in order not to weary you further, I wouldrequest that you are kind enough to hear us briefly.

RIGHT: But in order not to weary you further, I wouldrequest that you <u>be</u> kind enough to hear us briefly.

WRONG: The recommendation that school teachers are evaluated for stipend every year was approved.

RIGHT: The recommendation that school teachers <u>be evaluated</u> for stipend every year was approved.

PRACTICE TEST

Test 1. SENTENCE COMPLETION: Choose the CORRECT answer.

1. The proposal that our downtown college bookstore _____ on Sundays was welcomed.

   A. stays open

B. stay open

2. Everybody liked my suggestion that Gordon McDonald _____.

   A. is running for the next President of the United States

   B. run for the next President of the United States

Test 2. SENTENCE CORRECTION: Choose the INCORRECT word or phrase and CORRECT it.

1. He complied with the requirement that all graduate students in education should write a thesis.

2. The committee refused the request that the prerequisite shall be waived.

3. She ignored the suggestion that she gets more exercise.

4. The terrorist's demand that the airline provides a plane will not be met by the deadline.

5. He regretted not having followed his advisor's recommendation that he dropping the class.

ANSWER KEY

Test 1:

1. B (Here the simple form of the verb *stay* should be used after the noun *proposal* derived from subjunctive verb *propose*.)

2. B (Here the simple form of the verb *run* must be used even if it is in the third person singular.)

Test 2:

1. He complied with the requirement that all graduate students in education <u>write</u> a thesis.

2. The committee refused the request that the prerequisite <u>be waived</u>.

3. She ignored the suggestion that she <u>get</u> more exercise.

4. The terrorist's demand that the airline <u>provide</u> a plane will not be met by the deadline.

5. He regretted not having followed his advisor's recommendation that he <u>drop</u> the class.

LESSON 9

TESTING POINT: INVERT THE SUBJECT AND VERB WITH CONDITIONALS

ERROR EXAMPLE

WRONG: When a lovely woman says you look like her fiance, it means was she not engaged, you'd be able to win her love.

RIGHT: When a lovely woman says you look like her fiance, it means <u>were</u> she not engaged, you'd be able to win her love.

GRAMMAR GUIDE

The inversion of the subject and verb in conditional structures occurs when the helping verb in the conditional clause is *had, should,* or *were,* and the conditional connector *if* is omitted.

WRONG: Had Mary Lincoln know how much pernicious mischief Herndon would perpetrate in later years, she would have been more self-serving.

RIGHT: <u>Had</u> Mary Lincoln <u>known</u> how much pernicious mischief Herndon would perpetrate in later years, she would have been more self-serving.

WRONG: I would definitely help you was I in a position to help.

RIGHT: I would definitely help you <u>were</u> I in a position to help.

PRACTICE TEST

Test 1. SENTENCE COMPLETION: Choose the CORRECT answer.

1. Had you studied harder, your test score should be higher.

   A. would have been higher

   B. should be higher

2. Had it not been for your invaluable assistance with my application, _____.

   A. I would not have been accepted by Harvard Law School

   B. I would not be accepted by Harvard Law School

Test 2. SENTENCE CORRECTION: Choose the INCORRECT word or phrase and CORRECT it.

1. Was she there, she would make a speech at the university.

2. Has there been a chance, I would have taken it.

3. Lost your job, what would you have done?

4. Had they asked me, I would give my opinion yesterday.

5. Had Bob study more, he would have passed the test.

ANSWER KEY

Test 1:

1. A (Here past future perfect tense *would have been* should be used because in the inverted adverbial clause of condition, past perfect tense *had...studied* is used.)

2. A (In the conditional clause, we used past perfect tense, therefore, in the main clause, we should use past future perfect tense: *would not have been accepted.*)

Test 2:

1. <u>Were</u> she there, she would make a speech at the university.

2. <u>Had</u> there <u>been</u> a chance, I would have taken it.

3. <u>Had</u> you <u>lost</u> your job, what would you have one?

4. Had they asked me, I <u>would have given</u> my opinion yesterday.

5. <u>Had</u> Bob <u>studied</u> more, he would have passed the test.

LESSON 10

TESTING POINT:

ERRORS WITH VERBALS

ERROR EXAMPLE

WRONG: It was the task of all interesting nations to make sure this new state of affairs did not spill over into tension – or worse.

RIGHT: It was the task of all <u>interested</u> nations to make sure this new state of affairs did not spill over into tension – or worse.

GRAMMAR GUIDE

Verbals are participles, gerunds, and infinitives. They can be used as adjectives.

For present participles, they end with *–ing*; for past participles, they end with *–ed*.

When modifying nouns, present participles tend to have active meaning whereas past participles have passive meaning.

WRONG: The millionaire's stealing Land Rover was finally recovered with the help of the police.

RIGHT: The millionaire's <u>stolen</u> Land Rover was finally recovered with the help of the police.

Gerunds are verbal nouns. They end in *–ing* like the present participle. They can be used as the subjects of verbs, the objects of prepositions and certain verbs.

WRONG: Young people should always look forward to see miracles happen in their lives.

RIGHT: Young people should always look forward to <u>seeing</u> miracles happen in their lives.

Infinitives are formed with *to* plus the simple form of the verb. They can be used as the subjects of verbs and the objects of certain verbs.

WRONG: John Glenn was the first American orbiting the Earth.

RIGHT: John Glenn was the first American <u>to orbit</u> the Earth.

PRACTICE TEST

Test 1. SENTENCE COMPLETION: Choose the CORRECT answer.

1. The exhausting basketball players were too tired to move after they had won the championship.

   A. exhausting

   B. exhausted

2. Tenants of this building are advised to shut the windows in winter; for we_____.

   A. can not afford heating the outside

   B. can not afford to heat the outside

Test 2. SENTENCE CORRECTION: Choose the INCORRECT word or phrase and CORRECT it.

1. This new sports car is very easy driving.

2. The most important discovery knowing to all might be DNA.

3. No rich person can afford feeding such a hungry nation after the war.

4. Have finished dinner, we took a walk along the Thames.

5. No one looks forward to hear bad news after the college entrance exam.

ANSWER KEY

Test 1:

1. B (Here *exhausted* should be used because it is a past participle used as an adjective and it has a passive meaning.)

2. B (Here after *afford*, an infinitive *to heat* must be used instead of a gerund.)

Test 2:

1. This new sports car is very easy to drive.

2. The most important discovery known to all might be DNA.

3. No rich person can afford *to* feed such a hungry nation after the war.

4. Having finished dinner, we took a walk along the Thames.

5. No one looks forward to hearing bad news after the college entrance exam.

LESSON 11

TESTING POINT:

PROBLEMS WITH INFINITIVES

ERROR EXAMPLE

WRONG: For example, if we decide to play blackjack, the first thing doing is decide how much we are going to wager or risk.

RIGHT: For example, if we decide to play blackjack, the first thing <u>to do</u> is decide how much we are going to wager or risk.

GRAMMAR GUIDE

Infinitives are formed with *to* plus the simple form of the verb.

They can be used as the subjects of verbs and the objects of certain verbs.

WRONG: Johny got lost in New York City because he forgot reading the direction on the tourist map.

RIGHT: Johny got lost in New York City because he forgot to read the direction on the tourist map.

Infinitives can be used as adjective phrases after noun phrases.

WRONG: Jack Daniel was the only man receiving this privilege

RIGHT: Jack Daniel was the only man to receive this privilege.

Infinitives can also be used to show purpose.

WRONG: He is learning Chinese for finding a job in China.

RIGHT: He is learning Chinese to find a job in China.

PRACTICE TEST

Test 1. SENTENCE COMPLETION: Choose the CORRECT answer.

1. The first man_____on the moon was Neil Armstrong.

A. landing

B. to land

2. _____on the college entrance test, we must study hard and be fully prepared.

A. To get a higher score

B. Getting a higher score

Test 2. SENTENCE CORRECTION: Choose the INCORRECT word or phrase and CORRECT it.

1. She is reputed to be a spy for KGB during the Cold War.

2. The injured worker was reported to die the day before.

3. They chose to not have attended the meeting.

4. Our job is help you to pass the standardized exam.

5. The police officer offered give her a ride home because she was drunk.

ANSWER KEY

Test 1:

1. B (Here we use infinitive *to land* instead of the present participle *landing* because *to land on the moon* functions as an adjective phrase to modify the noun before it.)

2. A (here an infinitive *to get*... must be used as the adverbial of purpose)

Test 2:

1. She is reputed <u>to have been</u> a spy for the KGB during the Cold War.

2. The injured worker was reported <u>to have died</u> the day before.

3. They chose <u>not to attend</u> the meeting.

4. Our job is <u>to help</u> you to pass the standardized exam.

5. The police officer offered <u>to give</u> her a ride home because she was drunk.

CHAPTER FIVE

ADVERB/ADJECTIVE CONFUSION

LESSON 12

TESTING POINT: USE BASIC ADJECTIVES AND ADVERBS CORRECTLY

ERROR EXAMPLE

WRONG: Due to the island's'healing'powers the baby will grow abnormal faster and be born in a few weeks.

RIGHT: Due to the island's'healing'powers the baby will grow <u>abnormally</u> faster and be born in a few weeks.

GRAMMAR GUIDE

In English, adjectives and advrbs have different functions in a sentence. Basically, an adjective is used to modify a noun or a pronoun.

WRONG: Modern art is on display at the Guggenhein Museum, a building with an unusually design.

RIGHT: Modern art is on display at the Guggenhein Museum, a building with an <u>unusual</u> design.

An adverb is used to modify a verb, an adjective or another adverb.

WRONG: Our offshore telephone call centres were successful established in 2005.

RIGHT: Our offshore telephone call centres were <u>successfully</u> established in 2005.

WRONG: I worked real hard on Microeconomics, but failed.

RIGHT: I worked <u>really hard</u> on Microeconomics, but failed.

PRACTICE TEST

Test 1. SENTENCE COMPLETION: Choose the CORRECT answer.

1. The newly released Hollywood movie tells an_____ moving story.

   A. extreme

   B. extremely

2. Mary Lopez got almost full marks on her biology final because she _____ for it.

   A. had studied very hardly

   B. had studied very hard

Test 2. SENTENCE CORRECTION: Choose the INCORRECT word or phrase and CORRECT it.

1. Jake was extreme happy to see her coming back from vacation in Africa.
2. The deadly silence of the night even scared bravest soldiers.
3. You must do it very carefully, if not perfect.
4. He worked very hardly on his college entrance exams.
5. You should order that book real soon.

ANSWER KEY

Test 1:

1. B (Here we must use *extremely* instead of *extreme* because extremely is an adverb of degree and it is here used to modify the adjexctive *moving*.)

2. B (Here *hard* must be used because *hardly* means *almost not*)

Test 2:

1. Jake was extremely happy to see her coming back from vacation in Africa.

2. The dead silence of the night even scared the bravest soldiers.

3. You must do it very carefully, if not perfectly.

4. He worked very hard on his college entrance exams.

5. You should order that book really soon.

CHAPTER SIX

INCORRECT USE OF A PREPOSITON

LESSON 13

TESTING POINT: RECOGNIZE INCORRECT PREPOSITIONS AND PREPOSITIONAL PHRASES

ERROR EXAMPLE

WRONG: Israel's Prime Minister Ehud Olmert said Israeli forces will abstain of attacking the Gaza Strip if militants stop firing rockets.

RIGHT: Israel's Prime Minister Ehud Olmert said Israeli forces will <u>abstain from</u> attacking the Gaza Strip if militants stop firing rockets.

GRAMMAR GUIDE

In English, single prepositions are easy to master, however, prepositional phrases are very hard to handle. A prepositional phrase consists of a preposition and an object.

WRONG: The young artist earns her living of painting pictures for tourists in the park.

RIGHT: The young artist earns her living <u>by painting pictures</u> for tourists in the park.

WRONG: You can always learn what mistakes you have made in your practice exercise to do better in the real exam.

RIGHT: You can always learn <u>from what mistakes you have made</u> in your practice exercise to do better in the real exam.

PRACTICE TEST

Test 1. SENTENCE COMPLETION: Choose the CORRECT answer.

1. I know that I can always_____you when I am in trouble at school.

   A. rely in

   B. rely on

2. Russell MacDonald finally_____me about setting up a branch office in Asia.

   A. agreed to

B. agreed with

Test 2. SENTENCE CORRECTION: Choose the INCORRECT word or phrase and CORRECT it.

1. I look forward for seeing you at the registration time.

2. Thomas has always been interested to sing at KTV.
3. We are very sorry to keep you here waiting..

4. He is very disappointed about his test score on the exam.

5. During the summer I usually work at my grandpa's snake farm.

ANSWER KEY

Test 1:

1. B (Here you should use *rely on* instead of *rely in*.)

2. B (*Agree with* is usually used with *somebody*. *Agree to* is usually followed by *something*.)

Test 2:

1. I look forward to seeing you at the registration time.

2. Thomas has always been interested in singing at KTV.

3. We are very sorry for keeping you here waiting.

4. He is very disappointed at his test score on the exam.

5. During the summer I usually work on my grandpa's snake farm.

LESSON 14

TESTING POINT: ERRORS WITH PREPOSITIONS

ERROR EXAMPLE

WRONG: As always, we welcome comments and suggestions from readers, and we look forward hearing what you think of this new product.

RIGHT: As always, we welcome comments and suggestions from readers, and we <u>look forward to</u> hearing what you think of this new product.

GRAMMAR GUIDE

Remember that being able to use prepositions correctly will definitely help you score a few points higher on the test, therefore, you should always try to memorize the use of the most frequently tested prepositions. The following are some typical examples:

Between and *among*: *between* is used with two nouns, or persons or things, *among* is used among three nouns or persons or things.

WRONG: John Obama is the tallest between the boys in my class.

RIGHT: John Obama is the tallest among the boys in my class.

But and *except:* they have the same kind of use, however never confuse *except* with *excepting* or *exception*.

WRONG: No one excepting Cathy knows much about our secret.

RIGHT: No one but Cathy knows much about our secret.

Instead of and *Instead:* remember that never confuse *instead of* with *instead*. *Instead of* is a phrasal preposition whereas *instead* is an adverb.

WRONG: But more than half revealed that they intended to send an electronic greeting card, instead a traditional one

RIGHT: But more than half revealed that they intended to send an electronic greeting card, instead of a traditional one.

PRACTICE TEST

Test 1. SENTENCE COMPLETION: Choose the CORRECT answer.

1. He always looks up to those who are senior to him in rank, and looks down at those who are junior to him in rank.

   A. looks down at

   B. looks down upon

2. To lead a well-balanced life, you need_____.

   A. to have other interests beside studying

   B. to have other interests besides studying

Test 2. SENTENCE CORRECTION: Choose the INCORRECT word or phrase and CORRECT it.

1. The next performance begins in dusk.

2. These toys are made with the Indians living in Northern Alberta.

3. Joyce is quite satisfied by his new apartment downtown.

4. The students are bored for sitting all day in the classroom.

5. What time do you think you will arrive to Boston?

ANSWER KEY

Test 1:

1. B (Here you should use *look down upon* instead of *look down at*; for they have totally different meaning.)

2. B (*besides* means *in addition to,* never confuse *besides* with *beside*)

Test 2:

1. The next performance begins <u>at</u> dusk.

2. These toys are made <u>by</u> the Indians living in Northern Alberta.

3. Joyce is quite satisfied <u>with</u> his new apartment downtown.

4. The students are bored <u>with</u> sitting all day in the classroom.

5. What time do you think you will arrive <u>in</u> Boston?

CHAPTER SEVEN

FAULTY DICTION

LESSON 15

TESTING POINT: USE *BORROW* AND *LEND, LET* AND *LEAVE* CORRECTLY

ERROR EXAMPLE

WRONG: The interest rate was meant to be a floor on market interest rates; no bank would borrow in the markets for less than it could get at the Fed.

RIGHT: The interest rate was meant to be a floor on market interest rates; no bank would <u>lend</u> in the markets for less than it could get at the Fed.

GRAMMAR GUIDE

The words *borrow* and *lend* seem to be similar, but completely different in meaning. To *borrow* means to take something from somebody and give it back, but to *lend* is to give something to somebody and take it back.

WRONG: The crops are dying out because there is a little rain this summer.

RIGHT: The crops are dying out because there is little rain this summer.

As for *a few* and *few*, *a few* means some, whereas *few* means *almost not any*. Both of them modify countable nouns.

WRONG: Pamela feels very lonely on the weekend; for she has a few friends in Los Angeles.

RIGHT: Pamela feels very lonely on the weekend; for she has <u>few</u> friends in Los Angeles.

To let and to *leave* sound similar, but similar in meaning. *To let* means to allow or to permit.

WRONG: Our English teacher allows us speak no other language but English both in class and at home.

RIGHT: Our English teacher lets us speak no other language but English both in class and at home.

To leave means to let someone or something remain, and it also means *to go* or *to depart*.

WRONG: Joyce let her cell phone on the airplane yesterday.

RIGHT: Joyce left her cell phone on the airplane yesterday.

PRACTICE TEST

Test 1. SENTENCE COMPLETION: Choose the CORRECT answer.

1. Small companies can lend money from the banks to either expand or consolidate their business.

   A. lend

   B. borrow

2. Before you leave for Paris, please_____ if you need anything.

   A. let me to know

B. let me know

Test 2. SENTENCE CORRECTION: Choose the INCORRECT word or phrase and CORRECT it.

1. Stan had an accident while he was driving the car that his cousin had borrowed him.

2. Would you please borrow me your pen?

3. Can I lend this dictionary for a few minutes while I check my composition?

4. Although her doctor allowed her family to visit her, he wouldn't leave anyone else go into her room.

5. You can let your car in long-term parking until you come back.

ANSWER KEY

Test 1:

1. B (Here you should use *borrow* instead of *lend* here because they have totally different meaning.)

2. B (*let* somebody *do* something, never put *to* in front of the simple verb)

Test 2:

1. Stan had an accident while he was driving the car that his cousin had lent him.

2. Would you please <u>lend</u> me your pen?

3. Can I <u>borrow</u> this dictionary for a few minutes while I check my composition?

4. Although her doctor allowed her family to visit her, he wouldn't <u>let</u> anyone else go into her room.

5. You can <u>leave</u> your car in long-term parking until you come back.

LESSON 16

TESTING POINT: USE *A LITTLE* AND *LITTLE*, *A FEW* AND *FEW* CORRECTLY

ERROR EXAMPLE

WRONG: In an attempt to add a few greenery to the concrete, many city roofs have been converted into gardens.

RIGHT: In an attempt to add <u>a little</u> greenery to the concrete, many city roofs have been converted into gardens.

GRAMMAR GUIDE

The difference between *a little* and *little* is that *a little* means some; whereas *little* means *almost not any*. Both of them modify uncountable nouns.

WRONG: The crops are dying out because there is a little rain this summer.

RIGHT: The crops are dying out because there is <u>little</u> rain this summer.

As for *a few* and *few, a few* means *some* whereas *few* means *almost not any*. Both of them modify countable nouns.

WRONG: Pamela feels very lonely on the weekend; for she has a few friends in Los Angeles.

RIGHT: Pamela feels very lonely on the weekend; for she has <u>few</u> friends in Los Angeles.

PRACTICE TEST

Test 1. SENTENCE COMPLETION: Choose the CORRECT answer.

1. _____ is currently available as to whether the governor will resign after the bribery scandal.

A. Few information

B. Little information

2. I am sure I will get a very high score this time because I made _____ on the exam.

A. only a little mistakes

B. only a few mistakes

Test 2. SENTENCE CORRECTION: Choose the INCORRECT word or phrase and CORRECT it.

1. Give me little butter, please.

2. We have a little news about the plane crash.

3. There are few tickets left for the concert.

4. A few people in my apartment building are friendly.

5. She speaks a little French.

ANSWER KEY

Test 1:

1. B (Here you should use *little* instead of *few* because information is an uncountable noun, therefore, it must be modified by *little*.)

2. B (Here *mistake* is a countable noun, therefore, *a few* should be used.)

Test 2:

1. Give me a little butter, please.

2. We have little news about the plane crash.

3. There are a few tickets left for the concert.

4. Few people in my apartment building are friendly.

5. She speaks little French.

CHAPTER EIGHT

NON-STANDARD WORDS, EXPRESSIONS, OR IDIOMS

LESSON 17

TESTING POINT: CHECK WORD FORM: WORDS THAT DON'T EXIST IN ENGLISH

ERROR EXAMPLE

WRONG: If you do not know whether your document contains hidden text, you can use the Document Inspectator to search for it.

RIGHT: If you do not know whether your document contains hidden text, you can use the Document <u>Inspector</u> to search for it.

GRAMMAR GUIDE

In English tests,, a word that does not exist in English is sometimes used to confuse you. However, these non-standard words are closely related to real English word forms. The following are a few of the most common examples:

WRONG: George Vancouver may not have been the first explorator who have discovered Vancouver.

RIGHT: George Vancouver may not have been the first <u>explorer</u> who have discovered Vancouver.

WRONG: The current estable situation is very good for the economy.

RIGHT: The current <u>stable</u> situation is very good for the economy.

WRONG: When we travel abroad, we need to bring a universal adaptator for our laptops and cell phones.

RIGHT: When we travel abroad, we need to bring a universal <u>adaptor</u> for our laptops and cell phones.

PRACTICE TEST

Test 1. SENTENCE COMPLETION: Choose the CORRECT answer.

1. The_____ sought refuge at the U.S. Embassy in Paris.

   A. defectator

   B. defector

2. It is very easy to recycle plastic, just take it to your local _____.

   A. plastic collection point

   B. plastical collection point

Test 2. SENTENCE CORRECTION: Choose the INCORRECT word or phrase and CORRECT it.

1. The commandor ordered the soldiers to march on.

2. We should give our consentment to the proposal.

3. The economer predicted the crash of the stock market.

4. What you have just said is absolutely ture.

5. The political commentater is optimistic about the presidential election.

ANSWER KEY

Test 1

1. B (Here you must use *defector* instead of *defectator* because there is no such word in English.)

2. A (Here you must use *plastic* instead of *plastical* because there is no such word as *plastical* in English.)

Test 2:

1. The <u>commander</u> ordered the soldiers to march on.

2. We should give our <u>consent</u> to the proposal.

3. The <u>economist</u> predicted the crash of the stock market.

4. What you have just said is absolutely <u>true</u>.

5. The political <u>commentator</u> is optimistic about the presidential election.

CHAPTER NINE

INCORRECT DEGREE OF COMPARISON

LESSON 18

TESTING POINT: CHECK EQUATIVE, COMPARATIVE, AND SUPERLATIVE DEGREE

ERROR EXAMPLE

WRONG: Perhaps more than any place in Asia, Hong Kong's energy comes from a powerful relationship with the present.

RIGHT: Perhaps more than <u>any other</u> place in Asia, Hong Kong's energy comes from a powerful relationship with the present.

GRAMMAR GUIDE

There are three kinds of comparison in English. They are the equative, comparative, and the superlative.

Equative degree is used to show equality.

WRONG: This building is as tall like that one by the seaside.

RIGHT: This building is <u>as </u>tall <u>as</u> that one by the seaside.

The comparative degree is used to compare two things that are not equal. In your test, when you see the word *more*, look for *than*.

WRONG: Michael is definitely more smarter than Jack Daniels.

RIGHT: Michael is definitely <u>smarter</u> than Jack Daniels.

The superlative degree is used to compare three or more things that are not equal. When you see the words like *one of the*, look for *most* or a word ending in *–est*.

WRONG: One of the most exciting thing for parents is a baby's first word spoken like a miracle..

RIGHT: <u>One of</u> the most exciting <u>things</u> for parents is a baby's first word spoken like a miracle.

PRACTICE TEST

Test 1. SENTENCE COMPLETION: Choose the CORRECT answer.

1. Vancouver is more beautiful_____ in the world.

   A. than any city

   B. than any other city

2. He is the _____ person in the class to be late.

   A. least possible

   B. less possible

Test 2. SENTENCE CORRECTION: Choose the INCORRECT word or phrase and CORRECT it.

1. Our building is the same height like yours.

2. Jennifer is definitely smart as Marilyn.

3. The population of my hometown is much smaller than Shanghai.

4. The higher the degree you have, the more high wage you will get.

5. One of the most difficult problem in math is logical reasoning.

ANSWER KEY

Test 1:

1. B (Here you should use *than any other city* instead of *than any city* because any city includes Vancouver itself.)

2. A (Here you should use *least* because there must be at least three or more students in a class.)

Test 2:

1. Our building is <u>the same </u>height *as* yours.

2. Jennifer is definitely <u>as</u> smart <u>as</u> Marilyn.

3. The population of my hometown is much smaller than<u> that of</u> Shanghai.

4. The higher the degree you have, the<u> higher</u> the wage you will get.

5. One of the most difficult <u>problems</u> in math is logical reasoning.

LESSON 19

TESTING POINT:

COMPARATIVE ESTIMATES:

-*MORE THAN* AND *LESS THAN*

ERROR EXAMPLE

WRONG: After the last summit the financial markets' enthusiasm over the ludicrous idea of a leveraged EFSF evaporated after fewer than 48 hours.

RIGHT: After the last summit the financial markets' enthusiasm over the ludicrous idea of a leveraged EFSF evaporated after <u>less than</u> 48 hours.

GRAMMAR GUIDE

More than or *less than* is used before a specific number to express an estimate that may be *a little more* or *a little less* than the number.

WRONG: To underline his point, he said it has taken the U.S. more than 200 year to get to its current state of democracy.

RIGHT: To underline his point, he said it has taken the U.S. more than 200 years to get to its current state of democracy.

WRONG: Nancy has more than twenty apartments downtown, but she has few than ten thousand dollars in her bank account.

RIGHT: Nancy has more than twenty apartments downtown, but she has less than ten thousand dollars in her bank account.

PRACTICE TEST

Test 1. SENTENCE COMPLETION: Choose the CORRECT answer.

1. He said that the company had_____, but he declined to comment further.

   A. more than a hundred employee

   B. more than a hundred employees

2. In the Longwood Garden, you can see_____a thousand kinds of flowers and exotic plants.

   A. more than

   B. many

Test 2. SENTENCE CORRECTION: Choose the INCORRECT word or phrase and CORRECT it.

1. More one hundred people came to the meeting.

2. We have lived in the United States for as less than seven years.

3. The main library has more as one million volumes.

4. A new shopping center on the north side will have five hundred shops more than.

5. There are most than fifty students in the lab, but only two computers.

ANSWER KEY

Test 1:

1. B (Here you should use *employees* instead of *employee* because after more than + a specific number, you should the plural noun.)

2. A (here *more than* should be used because we have a specific number *a thousand kinds*)

Test 2:

1. <u>More than one hundred</u> people came to the meeting.

2. We have lived in the United States for <u>less than seven years</u>.

3. The main library has <u>more than one million</u> volumes.

4. A new shopping center on the north side will have <u>more than five hundred</u> shops.

5. There are <u>more than fifty</u> students in the lab, but only two computers.

CHAPTER TEN

CONFUSION BETWEEN WORDS WITH SIMILAR SOUNDS (HOMOPHONES OR NEAR-HOMOPHONES)

LESSON 20

TESTING POINT:

USE WORDS WITH SIMILAR SOUNDS CORRECTLY

ERROR EXAMPLE

WRONG: Elinor agreed to it all, for she did not think he deserved the complement of rational opposition.

RIGHT: Elinor agreed to it all, for she did not think he deserved the <u>compliment</u> of rational opposition.

GRAMMAR GUIDE

In English, words with similar sounds are called homophones or homonyms. They look alike or sound alike (or both) but have very different meanings. The following are the most common homophones you should try to remember:

accept/except

advice/advise

allusion/illusion

by/buy/bye

capital/capitol

complement/compliment

council/counsel

discreet/discrete

dual/duel

elicit/illicit

eminent/imminent

fair/fare

lie/lye

meat/meat/mete

role/roll

scene/seen

stationary/stationery

whine/wine

WRONG: In the dual of hope and disappointment ,if you grasp hope with your firm and courageous hands , the victory will certainly belong to you.

RIGHT: In the duel of hope and disappointment ,if you grasp hope with your firm and courageous hands , the victory will certainly belong to you.

.**WRONG**: Dr. Johnson is one of the most imminent scholars on Romanticism in this century.

RIGHT: Dr. Johnson is one of the most eminent scholars on Romanticism in this century.

.**WRONG**: One of our favorite things to do as children was to role snowballs down hills to see how much speed they could pick up.

RIGHT: One of our favorite things to do as children was to roll snowballs down hills to see how much speed they could pick up.

PRACTICE TEST

Test 1. SENTENCE COMPLETION: Choose the CORRECT answer.

1. Sharon's remark of someone_____ really annoyed her

boss.

   A. excepting bribery

   B. accepting bribery

2. "Women cannot and _____," she said, before telling a fraudulent tale of shopping and false price tags.

   A. do not lye

   B. do not lie

Test 2. SENTENCE CORRECTION: Choose the INCORRECT word or phrase and CORRECT it.

1. She was too discrete to mention the money in front of her mother.

2. The police illicited the truth from her family.

3. Without stationary we would not be able to do our job at all.

4. We don't have enough capitol to expand to Asia now.

5. A survey by The Sleep Counsel showed a quarter of men never wake up in a bad mood, compared to just one in seven women

ANSWER KEY

Test 1:

1. B (Here you should use *accepting* instead of *excepting* because there is no such use as *excepting something* in English.)

2. B (*Lye* and *lie* have totally different meanings: *lye* is a strong alkaline substance whereas *lie* means telling something that is not true.)

Test 2:

1. She was too <u>discreet</u> to mention the money in front of her mother.

2. The police <u>elicited</u> the truth from her family.

3. Without <u>stationery</u> we would not be able to do our job at all.

4. We don't have enough <u>capital</u> to expand to Asia now.

5. A survey by The Sleep <u>Council</u> showed a quarter of men never wake up in a bad mood, compared to just one in seven women

ACKNOWLEDGEMENTS

The author would like to thank his colleagues and students for bring some of these mistakes to life.

The author and publisher are grateful to those who have made this publication possible by providing all kinds of support from editing, graphic design, and proof-reading. Efforts have been made to identify the source of materials used in this book, however, it has not always been possible to identify the sources of all the materials used, or to trace the copyright holders. If any omissions are brought to our attention, we will be happy to include the appropriate aknowlegements on reprinting.

ABOUT THE AUTHOR

Dr. Richard Lee is a professor of English and distinguished publishing scholar with more than ten books published under his name. His books are available on Amazon, other online stores, and in bookstores worldwide. Dr, Lee pursued his graduate education at the University of Rochester and the University of British Columbia and got his Ph.D. in English. Dr. Lee lives in beautiful Vancouver, British Columbia.

www.ingramcontent.com/pod-product-compliance
Lightning Source LLC
Chambersburg PA
CBHW071734110426
42739CB00043B/3131